THE
VICTORIA
WALKING GUIDE

· OLD TOWN · CHINATOWN ·
THE WATERFRONT · JAMES BAY

Rosemary Neering

WHITECAP BOOKS
Vancouver / Toronto

Copyright © 1994 by Rosemary Neering
Whitecap Books Ltd.
Vancouver/Toronto

Edited by Elizabeth McLean
Cover design by Warren Clark
Interior design by Susan Doering
Maps by Stuart Daniel, Starshell Maps
Cover photograph by Al Harvey
Interior photographs are by the author, except as noted. Archival photographs
courtesy of the British Columbia Archives and Records Service (BCARS).
Typeset by CryptoGraphics

Printed and bound in Canada.

Canadian Cataloguing in Publication Data

Neering, Rosemary, 1945–
    The Victoria walking guide

    ISBN 1-55110-171-8
    1. Victoria (B.C.)—Guidebooks. 2. Walking—British Columbia—Victoria—
Guidebooks. I. Title.
FC3846.18.N44 1994   917.11'28   C94-910011-0
F1089.5.V6N44 1994

CONTENTS

ACKNOWLEDGEMENTS

THANKS TO THE footsore—Bern and Cathy Atkins and Bob Harrison—who check-walked some or all of the routes. Special thanks to John Sansom, for information, walking, photography, and guidance. And thank you to Joe Thompson, for his help and support.

INTRODUCTION

ON THE CORNER of Bastion and Government, a blues guitarist belts out a lusty tune for the passers-by. He could not have chosen a more central or more historic spot. He busks halfway between Victoria's Parliament Buildings and Chinatown, two short blocks from the waterfront, a few metres from the site of Fort Victoria's northeast bastion. Here, prospectors on their way to the Cariboo gold rush eagerly sought saloons or outfitters, and sober bankers considered fiscal futures amid palatial surroundings in the town's golden decade after 1900. And he's looking the part: his bushy whiskers, flowing cape, and broad hat would have done a prospector proud. If he would just promise to stay there, we could put him on the map of this downtown Victoria walking tour.

But no matter that he'll soon be gone. The history, the low-rise Victorian streetscape, and the modern restorations that make walking Victoria's central core a pleasure will remain.

These blocks from the Parliament Buildings to Chinatown, east from the harbour waterfront, were the centre of Victoria from the town's first days to the First World War. In 1843, the Hudson's Bay Company (HBC) anticipated the cession of the Oregon Territory to the United States by building Fort Victoria as the company's new northwest coast headquarters. For the next fifteen years, the life of the traders, the few settlers who came to join them, and the Coast Salish Songhees who moved to land across the harbour centred on the world within the pickets of the fort.

In 1858, as news of gold found on the Fraser River sped round the world, that life ended forever. Some twenty thousand prospectors crowded into Fort Victoria, their last major stopping place en route to the gold. Within a year, former HBC man and now full-time Vancouver Island governor James Douglas had sold the land the fort stood on to the highest bidders, the old fort buildings were demolished, and the new buildings of Victoria were rapidly rising.

Though bedevilled by occasional recessions and setbacks, Victoria continued to prosper and expand through the 1860s, 1870s, and 1880s, bolstered by the decision that it would be the capital for the melded colonies that made up British Columbia. The town grew north and south from the area of the fort, between Bastion and Broughton streets. Douglas encouraged growth to the south by having the Parliament Buildings constructed in

Victoria's Inner Harbour in its busiest days, ca. 1912, with a CPR steamship on the left, a Grand Trunk Pacific steamship at its wharf on the right, and other harbour traffic. (BCARS 14522)

the James Bay area, and built one of the earliest houses in James Bay himself. He was soon followed by other families who chose to live in the relative quiet and spaciousness of Victoria's first suburb. To the north of the old fort grounds, hoteliers and saloonkeepers, shopkeepers, and professional men set up along the new streets, and Chinese immigrants created Canada's first and for many years largest Chinatown. Warehouses and wharves were constructed along Wharf Street, and a stream of goods and passengers came and went from the town.

The years after 1898 were the Old Town's best years.

Wharf Street, from the corner of Fort, already built up with warehouses in 1867. (BCARS 8735)

The impressive new Parliament Buildings opened in 1898, just as a new horde of would-be prospectors stopped by on their way to the Klondike gold rush. A spate of building changed the streetscape along Government and intersecting streets. The Canadian Pacific Railway built the Empress Hotel in 1907–8, the harbour became home port to most of the sealing fleet that plied north coast waters, steamers called here on the busy Victoria-Vancouver-Seattle run, and ships from the famous Empress line and deep-sea freighters tied up at the Outer Wharves.

Downtown's boom years ended in 1912. While the Old Town did not die, it certainly became sleepier as Victorians drove their new automobiles to new suburbs.

Through the 1940s and 1950s, the old buildings decayed. Only in the late 1960s and the decades that followed did the city turn back to its Old Town and Chinatown, with private and public restoration of the grand old buildings and creation of new public spaces.

This guide outlines a walking tour route that circles from the Parliament Buildings through Old Town to Chinatown and back along the harbour. Two other walks show off the best of old and modern Victoria. The Westsong/West Bay walk follows the northwest side of the harbour. The James Bay tour follows the waterfront along the busy Inner Harbour to Laurel Point, past Fishermen's Wharf to Victoria's most popular waterfront walkways, Beacon Hill Park, and the historic houses and modern apartment buildings of James Bay.

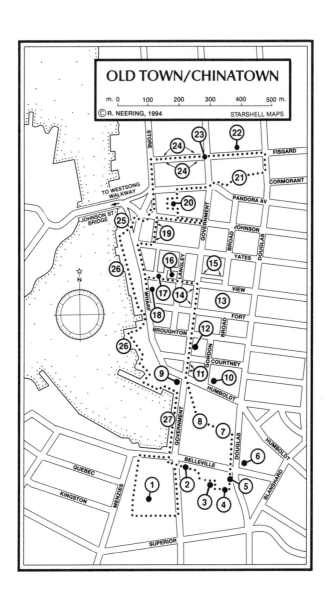

OLD TOWN/CHINATOWN

m. 0   100   200   300   400   500 m.

© R. NEERING, 1994   STARSHELL MAPS

THE OLD TOWN/ CHINATOWN TOUR

THIS WALKING TOUR is just a few kilometres in length, but can take anywhere from an hour to a full day. Since it is circular, you can begin anywhere; the directions start at the south end, near the Parliament Buildings. Most B.C. Transit buses stop downtown, on or near the tour route. You can park in downtown parking lots, including those run by the city. Watch for directional signs on major streets. Numbers in parentheses refer to the map on the facing page.

Parliament Buildings to Empress Hotel

Begin in front of the Parliament Buildings (1), across Belleville from the Inner Harbour, at the southwest corner of Belleville and Government streets. In 1859, as prospectors and would-be merchants crowded ashore below the Hudson's Bay fort, former HBC man and Vancouver Island governor James Douglas decided it would be profitable to sell off much of the land near the waterfront. The area beyond the muddy, smelly bay south of the fort he chose as the site, less desirable and therefore less valuable, for the colony's first legislative buildings, five "Birdcages," described as between Dutch toys and Chinese pagodas in style. In 1892, a smallpox epidemic all but closed Victoria's harbour, adding to the dire effects of an economic depression. To provide employment and boost the economy, the B.C. government decided to build new legislative buildings.

Francis Mawson Rattenbury, a twenty-five-year-old Englishman, scooped the design competition with his plans for three wings that met under a central dome thirteen metres in diameter. Local materials were used as much as possible in construction: granite from Nelson Island, slate from Jervis Inlet, andesite stone from Haddington Island five hundred kilometres away, "of a pearly grey colour, of a very transparent tone [which] takes on delicate and various shadings with each change of the sky."

Although the buildings did not open until 1898, they were first illuminated in 1897, to celebrate Queen Victoria's diamond jubilee. Various additions were made to the buildings between 1911 and 1916. Rattenbury went on to great fame as B.C.'s premier architect of public buildings, and to later infamy in England when he was murdered by his wife's young chauffeur-lover, a death in which his wife

A horse-drawn coach in front of the Parliament Buildings shortly after they opened. (BCARS 58562)

was implicated. She committed suicide; the young man was released after a number of years in prison.

The buildings are open to the public year-round, seven days a week in summer, weekdays from September to June. For details and times of tours call 387-3046. The tour takes about thirty minutes and includes information on the history of the buildings, the area, and the parliamentary system.

The lower rotunda in the main building features four quintessentially Victorian virtues: courage to initiate new ventures, represented by the meeting of George Vancouver and Juan Francisco de la Bodega y Quadra in 1792;

enterprise to organize, shown by the arrival of James Douglas to establish Fort Victoria; labour to transform dreams, shown in the building of Fort Victoria; and justice to maintain a way of life, shown by a court scene at Clinton, in the Cariboo.

Walk west on Belleville, away from Government Street, in front of the buildings. A war memorial to the dead of World Wars I and II and the Korean War is at the Government Street corner of the building lawn. Farther west are a statue of Queen Victoria and a totem pole. **Turn left just past the pole, and walk toward the buildings, then through the passageway that connects the west wing to the main building. Continue counterclockwise around the buildings.** High on the library wing, which protrudes from the main wing, are fourteen statues, by Vancouver sculptor Charles Marega, of men important in B.C. history, from Nuu-chah-nulth chief Maquinna to an assortment of politicians and explorers; check the cairn in front of the wing to identify the various mostly bearded frock-coated men. Also high on the building, as befits a library wing, are the faces of four writers, also identified on the cairn.

Follow the pathway behind the cairn to the Centennial Fountain, erected in 1958. The figures around the fountain represent the territories that made up British Columbia: the raven, for Vancouver Island; the eagle, for the Queen Charlotte Islands; the bear, for the colony of mainland B.C.; and the wolf, for the northern territory of Stickeen (Stikine).

Return to the corner of Government and Belleville, and cross Government Street, heading east. On your right is the provincial archives building, fronted by a carillon tower **(2)** built in 1967 as a gift to B.C. by people of Dutch origin who live in the province. The belfry contains forty-nine bronze bells cast in Holland, from the bourdon at 866 kilograms, to the smallest at nine kilograms. Seventy-five stairs wind through six complete circles to the carilloneur's position. The bells sound the quarter hours, with music played at noon and on special occasions.

Take a look at the changing photographic displays in the archives building entranceway. Native plant gardens border the walkways around the archives. A pamphlet available from the main museum building (tours are also available in the summer) describes the plants you'll see: wild grasses and sage from sand dunes; prickly pear cactus from the dry interior; heather from alpine regions; salal and sword fern from the coastal forest.

Continue east past the archives and turn right up the steps toward the main museum building (3). The massive glass showcases beside the building house totems and house fronts from native coastal villages, accompanied by archival photographs of those villages.

The Royal British Columbia Museum has garnered worldwide acclaim for its innovative and entertaining displays and dioramas. The First People's Gallery is a showpiece. In a Big House brought here from Alert Bay off northern Vancouver Island, sound and images convey an eerily accurate impression of native life on the coast. The modern history gallery presents life in nineteenth-century British Columbia. The natural history galleries take the visitor from the time of the woolly mammoth to the present, on the ground and under the sea.

The museum is open daily year-round; phone 387-3014 for hours and admission fees. Admission is free on winter Mondays.

Continue between the outdoor glass display cases and the museum building, then turn right and go up the paved incline behind the museum. Turn left to walk between Helmcken House and the St. Ann's Schoolhouse. Four Sisters of St. Ann, an order founded in Quebec in 1850 to work in country schools, came to Victoria in 1858 to establish a school for young ladies of all religions. These sisters and others who followed taught young women in Victoria and up the coast for many years. The schoolhouse, built as a cabin in Hudson's Bay Company squared-log style by company employee Jacques Lequechier in about 1845, is thought to be the oldest standing building in Victoria. It is now a school museum.

Helmcken House **(4)**, on your left, is probably the oldest house on its original site in the province, built in 1852 by John Sebastien Helmcken, Fort Victoria's first doctor and a pioneer politician, described by one writer as "the leading physician from San Francisco to the North Pole and from Asia to the Red River." Of course, at that time he may have been the only one. The original portion of the house was built of logs squared in the forest by Québecois employed by the HBC, floated to a bay near

Totems at Thunderbird Park, in front of Helmcken House.

this site, then hauled here by oxen. The house, restored, is open to the public.

Continue east, through the totem poles, across the grass toward Douglas Street. Thunderbird Park **(5)** was created in 1940 to display poles brought to Victoria from upcoast villages. A dozen years later, as the poles began to decay, replicas were made in the carving shed nearby and the originals stored in safety. The thunderbird, a central figure in native mythology, flaps its wings and thunder rumbles; lightning flashes from its eyes or from its belt, the lightning snake that sends harpoons from the sky.

Turn left on Douglas Street, and continue to the corner of Belleville. Native carvers continue to work in the carving shed beside the Mungo Martin House, to your left on Belleville, a Kwagiulth Big House that duplicates a house built at Fort Rupert before 1900. The potlatch dedicating the house lasted three days; it is now used for dancing, ceremonies, and other events.

Cross Belleville Street and walk north on Douglas Street. Across Douglas is the Crystal Garden **(6)**, a glass-covered pleasure palace built on a reinforced concrete raft atop a bog in the early 1920s. The Crystal, its seawater pool heated by steam from the next-door laundry, was the largest swimming pool in North America when it opened, *the* place to swim, dance, and flirt in the 1920s and 1930s. Wrote a commentator when it opened in 1925, "…under a great canopy of glass, there lies a large pool where swimmers disport themselves and on the encircling promenade, some distance above the water, people chat over tea at tables amid a profusion of shrubs, plants and flowers, while orchestral music floats above the laughter from below."

In 1964, the Canadian Pacific Railway (CPR) declined to renew its lease on the rapidly decaying building, and the city was forced to take it over. But the pool and building were simply too expensive to maintain, and in 1971 the last swimmer climbed from the water and the last dance notes sounded. The Crystal was boarded up. Just when it seemed it must be torn down and replaced by something more sterile, it was rescued and restored. The swimming pool area has become a conservatory, with tropical plants, birds, and animals; shops and a restaurant occupy the street frontage.

The Victoria Conference Centre proves a frame for the back of the Empress Hotel.

Walk north past the bus station on your left. Half-way along the block, turn in at the Victoria Conference Centre (7). (Wheelchair route: turn left on the sidewalk just past the bus station, and continue west, outside the conference centre, along the paths beside the Empress, then turn right to reach the front of the Empress Hotel.)

The two-level conference centre, opened in 1989, can accommodate more than fifteen hundred people in a lecture theatre, meeting rooms, and an assembly hall. Take a look inside at the paintings, outside at the plaza and fountains.

Continue through the conference centre into the Empress Hotel (8). "There is a view," wrote Rudyard

Kipling, passing through Victoria in 1907, "when the morning mist peels off the harbour where the steamers tie up, of the Houses of Parliament, on one hand, and a huge hotel on the other, which as an example of cunningly fitted-in waterfronts and facades is worth a very long journey." Kipling was impressed enough to declare Victoria, with Quebec City, one of Canada's two pillars of strength and beauty.

Kipling's words came of the city's and the CPR's dream to make Victoria a tourist destination. The CPR agreed to drain the tidal flats at James Bay and build a luxury hotel; citizens voted overwhelmingly to give the hotel major tax breaks. To lay the hotel's foundations, workmen drove pilings thirty-eight metres through the mud and ooze of the drying flats to bedrock. The main block of the Empress opened in 1908; the conservatory you are now in was part of a later addition.

Proceed through the Empress, stopping, if you like, for a drink in the Bengal Room, where an ex-tiger is pinned to the wall, evidence of a long-past empire. Afternoon tea in the main lobby has been a tradition since the hotel opened, although for a brief period light-fingered guests put paid to the use of silver tea sets.

The Empress has had good times and bad. During the Depression, the hotel offered its top-floor rooms at a dollar a night to older people—mostly women—who lived in increasing penury. Many are the tales of their economies: breakfast every other day, hot plates in the rooms, piano lessons offered to the public on the hotel's piano, bridge lessons given in the lobby. The city and the hotel recovered after World War II, but new hotel towers meant vigorous competition, and the Empress had to change some of its more endearing traditions. The death of one was probably little mourned: the hotel's electricity came from its own direct-current plant, and every evening, staff had to distribute radios and electric shavers to the guests. The hotel was refurbished in the 1960s, and again in 1989, when the conference centre was built.

Walk out the large front doors of the Empress, and turn right, past lawns, flowerbeds, and extravagantly garbed doormen, to the corner of Government and Humboldt streets.

The statue across Government Street, overlooking the Inner Harbour, is of Captain James Cook, who in 1776 was the first non-native known to have landed on Vancouver Island shores. Behind the statue, inset into the wall, are plaques honouring early arrivals in Victoria and the ships they sailed on.

Government Street to Bastion Square

From here on, you can choose to walk either side of Government Street, criss-crossing at corners as you please. Across Government Street, on the southwest corner of the intersection, a twenty-five-metre tall tower **(9)** supports a beacon that once flashed out across the harbour, welcoming aircraft that never came. The Sperry beacon, visible for a hundred kilometres, was to aid seaplanes that promoters hoped would land in the harbour at night. Even now, seaplanes do not use the harbour after dark.

The building under the beacon was once a gas station (with Spanish tile roofs on building and pumps). The lower floors were used for car repair and storage, convenient to the steamships and ferries that came and left from the harbour. It now houses the tourist information centre, a restaurant, and washrooms for boaters who dock nearby. You can pick up tourist literature and city maps here, or wait until you return at the end of this walking tour.

North and west lies the square kilometre of Old Town, centred on the region that was once Fort Victoria. Many of the buildings in this area date back to Victoria's boom times: a few survive from gold-rush days, some were built in the 1880s, and many come from the busy decade after 1900. The Government Street mall, from here north, was created in the 1960s, with brick sidewalks, one-way vehicle traffic, benches, planters, trees, and lighting. The globe lights and hanging baskets (twenty-six plants to each) have long been a feature of downtown streets.

Cross Humboldt Street. A block to your right on Humboldt (north side) is the Union Club **(10)**, long the last Victoria relic of the days when every gentleman had his club. For years, the club resisted admitting women, the old guard defeating each successive measure by increasingly smaller margins. In February 1994, the bastions fell:

members voted to let women join. Not overwhelmed with gratitude, most women questioned said they could see no reason to buy memberships in the club. The Union Club began in 1879; this building opened in 1912.

On the northwest corner of the Government-Humboldt intersection is the newer part of the customs and immigration building, dating from 1956. Behind it is the older part, opened in 1898, altered in 1914, a substantial reminder of the Dominion's presence in Victoria—and of Victoria's presence in the Dominion of Canada.

Matthew Macfie, writing in 1862, praised the macadamized streets, solid wooden footpaths, and substantial stone and brick warehouses of Victoria. A clergyman, he was considerably less enchanted by "drinking saloons, which abound vastly out of proportion to the wants of the population, [which] often supply entertainments of a low and vicious order, and they are much patronized." Macfie would understand the trauma induced by the never-ending question of where to put a downtown liquor store to serve tourists and office workers, but avoid panhandlers and alcohol abusers. After moving around the downtown area, the liquor store has come to rest in the customs building. Just round the corner is a newer phenomenon: a coffee bar. Five of these latte and cappuccino bars are said to have opened downtown in a single week early in 1994.

Some idea of the town's 1860s priorities can be garnered from the list of occupations Macfie presents, among them thirty-nine grocers, eighteen real estate agents, twenty-two restaurateurs, seventeen billiard hall keepers—and one plumber. A high percentage of these businesses were housed along Government Street, for the next fifty years Victoria's business centre.

Continue north on Government Street. On the northeast corner of Humboldt and Government, with its entrance on Humboldt Street, is the Belmont Building, one of the grandest erected in Victoria's boom years from 1908 to 1912. As you walk up Government Street **(11)**, glance back to see murals high above the street, on the back of the building. The American consulate was once next door (809–817 Government) in the Metropolitan Block, built in 1903.

Cross Courtney Street and continue north. At the northeast corner of Government and Courtney (901 Government) is what may be the oldest remaining brick building in Victoria—though it could scarcely be recognized as such. Now in mock-Tudor garb, it began life as the Victoria Hotel and continued for many years as the Windsor. It barely survived its Victoria Hotel days. Soon after gas mains were installed, the owner went looking for a gas leak, lighting his way with an unshielded candle. The resulting explosion wrecked the hotel interior and demolished a wall or two. The owner was badly singed.

Across the street is Harbour Square, opened in the 1970s as a downtown shopping mall. For whatever reason, it did not prosper, and is now occupied mainly by offices, with some stores at street level.

Just up from the old Windsor is a trio of buildings

Government Street in 1906, looking north from the corner of Broughton. (BCARS 14507)

(909–913 Government) intended as a single unit: the centre one, flat-faced, and two flanking bow-windowed façades built in 1893–94. The farthest north of these **(12)** houses a Victoria tradition. In 1916, Charles Rogers moved here from across the street, bringing with him his time-tested recipes for Rogers Chocolates. Although the recipe, the success, the leaded glass, the mosaic-tile floor, and the oak panelling have changed little, current shop assistants bear little resemblance to the eccentric Rogers and his wife Leah. After their only son shot himself at the age of fifteen, their eccentricity increased. They slept behind the shop, rising to make each day's chocolates well before dawn. Rogers chose whom he would sell to, and how many chocolates each could have. When exhaustion from overwork overtook the couple, they checked into hospital for a week's rest. After Charles died, Leah gave away most of the family money, and lived on a small pension until she died twenty-five years later.

The Weiler Building, on the corner of Broughton at 921 Government, was built in 1898, at the height of the Klondike gold rush. Imagine Victorians surging into the town's first department store, sighing at the art glass, Turkish carpets, fine china, silverware, and furniture from the Weiler furniture factory around the corner. Light spilled onto the displays through the large arched windows on first and second floors; at night, Victorians could gaze at the innovative lighted displays in the windows.

Cross Broughton Street and continue north on Government. The pickets of Fort Victoria extended north and west from this block. Look for the plaque between 1000 and 1006 Government (west side of the street) to see the exact location of the fort's corner, and for bricks inscribed with the names of fort pioneer residents in the sidewalk to see the fort outline.

Both sides of this block are lined with heritage buildings. On the east side: the Hamley Building, at 1001 Government, was built in 1870 (third and fourth floors added in 1887), in what was once the garden of Fort Victoria; an unnamed building at 1007 Government and the Greenwood Building at 1009–1013 Government were both built in about 1870; and the ca. 1880 building at 1017 Government was once the Albion Hotel. Look for Italianate features, such as round-headed windows and decorative roof lines adapted from styles popular along the American Pacific coast, whence came many of Victoria's nineteenth-century residents.

On the west side of the block are the Pemberton Holmes Building, at the corner of Broughton, built for a pottery company owner in 1899; and the Warner Building, built in 1905 at 1006 Government, once called the Promise Block, though prosaically for owner Oscar Promise. At 1022 Government, a year-round Christmas shop makes an ironic comment in what used to be the home of the Bank of British Columbia. The bank opened the doors of this Renaissance Italianate premises in 1886, serving customers from behind a solid mahogany counter. Poet Robert Service worked as a clerk in this office, almost overwhelmed by his princely salary of $50 a month after several years of near starvation. His job included sleeping in an apartment over the vault, with a loaded revolver on the bedside table, above a trap door to the vault. He was, he wrote, to "wake up at the smallest noise, to pop off possible burglars....after the first week it would have taken a charge of nitroglycerin to arouse me." Service hired a piano, bought a dinner jacket, and made the rounds of parties, dances, the theatre, and golf, resolving to abandon his dreams of adventure for life as a "nice fat little banker." A subsequent

Details from the Bank of British Columbia building, at Fort and Government streets.

posting to the Klondike in the middle of the gold rush restored his sanity. On this building is a plaque indicating where the main entrance to Fort Victoria was.

Cross Fort Street. North of Fort Street lies a contrast of old and new. The Eaton Centre **(13)**, ahead on the east side of Government, aroused more controversy than had any Victoria project for decades. When Eaton's decided to redevelop a site they or their predecessors had occupied for many years, the company planned to demolish the turn-of-the-century buildings on the site. Heritage activists protested, and the city and company negotiated. The ensuing discussions took several years. The end result, in front of you, combines new structures with heritage façades that were preserved and re-built on a new four-level mall and six-storey Eaton's building.

Although some heritage purists decry the faux heritage that surrounds the old façades, shoppers have voted with their wallets, and the mall, with the usual number of chain stores and a few local specialty stores, seems commercially successful. Circle the block to see if you can distinguish older façades from newer.

The west side of the 1100-block Government **(14)** is studded with heritage buildings that date from 1869 to 1908. At the corner, the Lascelles Block started as a one-storey general merchandise store in 1869, acquired a second storey in 1880, and shrank in 1908 when a bank was built next door. One of Canada's grandest bookstores now occupies that Edwardian classical Royal Bank building (1908) at 1108 Government. The external columns, arches, and cornices provide a nice foretaste of the carved wood, stone, bright banners, and book-shelves inside.

In the days when smoking was a gentleman's pleasure, the tobacconist's store of E.A. Morris (1116 Government, 1892) was a haven redolent with the smell of good cigars and the atmosphere of a Victorian club. Today, in fervently antismoking Victoria, its days as a tobacconist may be numbered. That would be a pity: change might endanger the Mexican onyx electrolier, its gas jet ever alight for the convenience of the smoker; the humidor; and the walk-in cabinet used to store cigars—though the mahogany panelling and mirrors on ceiling and walls should survive.

A plaque on the front of 69 Bastion Square (corner of Government and Bastion) notes the location of the northeast bastion of old Fort Victoria. A plaque on the building opposite explains the outline of the fort traced in the sidewalk. The blue-and-white building at 69 Bastion was Victoria's first law building, built in 1885 to house the city's law firms. Happily, the ground floor at the side of the building has been returned to its historic use as a pub.

Across from this building, still on the west side of Government, is the chateau-styled Bank of Montreal building, an 1896 design by Rattenbury. Like the Parliament Buildings, the bank is of Haddington Island stone. Completely fireproof, it contains no wood in its essential construction.

Look east across Government to see the 1910–14 Royal Trust building, and the start of Trounce Alley **(15)**, parallel to View Street. Businessman and landowner Thomas Trounce was infuriated in 1858 when the colonial administration sold the View Street right-of-way and the new owners fenced off their purchase, denying access to Trounce's Broad Street stores. Trounce built his own alley, closing it one day a year to maintain its status as private land. The alley became redundant when View was finally opened through to Government after a fire destroyed much of the block in 1910, but it remains as a privately owned thoroughfare.

From Government, turn left (toward the water) into

Bastion Square. Originally a street, then a parking lot, the wide walkway to Wharf Street was converted to a square featuring retail outlets in the late 1960s, with re-furbishment in 1993–94.

Cross Langley Street to enter the main part of the square (17). If Munich comes to mind when you view the turreted cream and blue-trimmed building on your right **(16)**, the former courthouse built in 1889, your instincts are on target: the design is probably based on a courthouse in the architect's native Munich. An ornate, open-cage elevator, said to be the oldest operational elevator in British Columbia, was installed because a chief justice had been warned by his doctor not to climb stairs.

The last court hearing took place here in 1962; the last public execution in Victoria took place in the square in the 1880s, when one Charlie Rogers was hanged for killing a fellow prison guard in New Westminster. In 1965, the building's present tenant, the Maritime Museum of B.C., moved in. Open daily (call 385-4222 for hours), the museum contains nautical artifacts from British Columbia's maritime history. Near the main entrance are plaques detailing the story of B.C.'s peripatetic pioneer judge, Matthew Baillie Begbie, and of the courthouse.

On the north side of the square past the museum is red-brick Burnes House, restored in 1967. Foreman of the volunteer firefighting Tiger Company, businessman Thomas J. Burnes was a familiar figure in 1880s Victoria, striding forth with his top hat, black cape, and gold-knobbed cane. Burnes came north from California in the

The Burnes block and Beaver Building, in Bastion Square.
(John Sansom photo)

1858 gold rush, but correctly judged his fortune lay in catering to would-be prospectors. Burnes House was one of the city's first luxury hotels, built in 1886, fashionable and successful until 1892, when the smallpox epidemic scared away business. The building then became a rooming house for lawyers and businessmen. As this area declined in the 1930s, it may have housed a brothel —a high-class one, of course. Next door is another of Burnes's projects, the 1867 Beaver Building.

Across the square is the former Law Chambers building, built in 1899 to house lawyers' offices, now used for stores and offices. Down the square on the same side is the 1892 Board of Trade building.

Wharf Street to Market Square

Continue to Wharf Street and turn left (south). From the earliest days of commercial Victoria, Wharf Street, aptly named, was the warehouse district, close to the docks on one side, and to stores, offices, and hotels on the other. The Wilson and Proctor warehouse (corner of Wharf and Bastion) was built in 1861. Look at the decorative detailing to see a caduceus, the wand carried by Hermes, the Greek god of commerce. The caduceus is also used as an emblem by the medical profession.

This warehouse and the ones next door at 1117–1121 Wharf housed the wholesaling operations of pioneer merchant R.P. Rithet, who also built the first outer wharves beyond Laurel Point. The decorative iron front on these buildings was ordered, prefabricated, from a foundry catalogue; two bays show the San Francisco maker's name and the date. The Rithet Building, 1117 Wharf **(18)**, was beautifully renovated by the provincial government in 1977 to house the tourism department. Walk into the lobby to see a well toward the back of the building, discovered by architects during renovations.

Next door to the Rithet Building, at 1107 Wharf, the Emily Carr Gallery has been suitably housed in a one-storey building where the artist's father, Richard Carr, once had his store. The public gallery displayed Carr paintings and drawings, but may be closed because of budget cuts. South of the gallery is the 1863 Odd Fellows building, once home to the first major fraternal organization in Victoria. Take a look at the modern carved wooden panel at the north end of the building.

Turn back (north) along Wharf Street. On both sides of Wharf north of Bastion Square are more warehouses and commercial buildings, now renovated, that date to between the 1860s and the turn of the century. The buildings on your right (east side of the street) were built around 1863, and housed a blacksmith, a wheelwright, and other businesses useful in a wholesale and shipping district.

Across the street is Hartwig Court, warehouses renovated in the 1970s to house restaurants and retail stores. What you see is the second storey of these buildings; the first floors are at ground level on the water side. The buildings at 1202 to 1214 Wharf went up in 1882, owned by Roderick Finlayson, a former chief factor for the Hudson's Bay Company who, like many others before and since, retired to Victoria. Early tenants were ships' chandlers and provisioners. The stone building at 1218 Wharf is the oldest on Wharf Street, thought to date back to 1858, beginning as a saloon and liquor warehouse. The iron front, granite lintels, and random-rubble construction survive; if the restaurant inside is open, take a peek at the interior that descends steeply to the waterfront. At the foot of Yates Street is a building that until recently housed a ships' chandler; look inside to see the heavy beams and old photographs.

Continue north on Wharf Street, cross Yates Street, and turn right (east) on Yates. In the 500 block of Yates are turn-of-the-century buildings that started life as hotels, warehouses, and retail premises. Walkers interested in Victorian commercial architecture should take a side trip up the block to see 534 Yates (Smith-Davidson-Leckie commercial building, 1900); 550–552 Yates (the Oriental Hotel, 1883/1888); 533 Yates (the American Hotel, ca. 1870); and 535 Yates (ca. 1900).

Return to the corner of Yates and Waddington Alley to see the Leiser Building (524 Yates, 1896). Wholesale grocer Simon Leiser installed in this building, a wonder in its day, two lines of track on each floor, leading to an elevator that contained a turntable, so that freight could be loaded or unloaded in any direction.

Turn north into Waddington Alley (19), beside the youth hostel building. A sign at the corner gives the history of the alley, the last remaining in the city with wooden paving blocks, recently augmented with modern wooden blocks.

Continue through the alley to Johnson Street. Saxon immigrant, miller, and baker Louis Wille opened a bakery in the building at the corner in 1887 and his descendants ran the bakery until it closed in 1976. The wheatsheaf sign of the baker survives on the building cornice.

Turn right and walk east up the south side of Johnson Street, to see one of the best heritage streetscapes in town. The buildings on your right were restored in the 1970s; 541–545 began as the Colonial Metropole Hotel in 1892; the Colonial House (551–555), also a hotel, was built in 1888; the Victoria Box and Paper Company building at 557–563 dates from 1890. All were in sad shape

—though with a certain decrepit charm—before restoration. Take a stroll into the Paper Box Arcade, an alleyway created by the restoration.

The buildings at 565 and 571–577 Johnson were built in about 1880. **Continue past them to Government Street, turn left and cross Johnson, then left again to return back down the north side of Johnson. Turn right halfway down the block, into Market Square (20).**

The development of Market Square in the mid-1970s rescued Victorian buildings that had deteriorated badly. The brightly painted Strand Hotel (550–554 Johnson) replaced the Strand Cafe and a brothel in 1892. The Milne Block (546–548 Johnson) opened as the Senator Hotel in 1891; the owner, A.R. Milne, was controller of Chinese

The Johnson Street buildings of Market Square.

entry for the Port of Victoria. Next door is the former Drake Hotel, built in 1894.

A ravine and creek once ran between Johnson and Pandora streets, dividing the Old Town from Chinatown. You can descend to the lower level of Market Square and look east, toward the parking lot, to see evidence of that ravine. The restored buildings on the north side of Market Square, facing Pandora, replaced wooden huts that housed Chinese immigrants until the early 1890s. The buildings at 515–527 Pandora went up in about 1895; they were used as shops and tenements. The B.C. Produce Building at 529 Pandora dates from 1875/1880.

Centennial Square to Chinatown

Go through Market Square to Pandora Street, on the north side of the square, and turn right on Pandora. Walk east to Government Street. The buildings across the street mark the beginning of modern Chinatown, which from the 1860s to 1920s housed up to three thousand people in six city blocks. **Cross Government, and turn left across Pandora.**

At the Government-Pandora corner is the McPherson Theatre. Performances in this building began in 1917, when Alexander Pantages opened the Orpheum Theatre with five acts that included Miss Ethel Davis and her fourteen Armstrong baby dolls, two comedy teams (one in blackface), a juggler, and a star of stage and silent screen. Legend swirls around Pantages: some say he made his stake in the Yukon, separating gold from the sawdust he swept from a saloon floor. He then came to Victoria, where he worked as a cook in a café. He later opened one by one the largest chain of vaudeville theatres in North America. But though he strove to adapt his theatres, the new movies spelled an end to his time as a theatre magnate. Depressed and ill, he is said to have taken to a semi-dark room in Victoria, where he summoned violinists to play for him.

Owner Thomas Shanks McPherson willed the building to the city in the 1960s. It was added to and substantially remodelled to open as the McPherson Theatre, complete with a baroque revival interior that features plaster cherubim.

Continue right on Pandora, then left just past the McPherson, into Centennial Square (21). Walk through the square past City Hall. The city closed a block of Cormorant Street and realigned Pandora to create this square in the 1960s. The fountain at its centre was a centennial gift to Victoria from neighbouring municipalities. Angry citizens halted construction on the first wing of City Hall —now facing Pandora Street—in 1878, protesting the building was an unnecessary extravagance. But it was completed, then added to in 1881 and 1891. The clock, with four 225-kilogram dials and 984-kilogram bell, was installed in 1891, after a long journey from England that saw it misdirected to the state of Victoria, in Australia.

Be careful as you look up at the hall—Centennial

Victoria's City Hall.

Square is home to rafts of starlings that cluster, especially at dusk, by the thousands on trees and buildings. City staff have tried to deter the birds with loud noises, the sound of a starling in distress, and a falconer and falcon —but the starlings are still winning, and the staff are still power-washing the sidewalks every morning.

Leave Centennial Square on the east side, by Douglas Street, and turn left (north) on Douglas. At the northeast corner of Douglas and Fisgard is the last physical presence of the company that founded Fort Victoria. The Hudson's Bay Company (known for many years simply as The Bay) store was under construction in 1914, put on hold by World War I, and completed in 1921.

On the northwest corner of the intersection is the

Masonic Temple built in 1878. Architect John Teague re-treated to Victoria after he panned and prospected for gold on the Fraser and in the Cariboo, stumbling out of the bush one winter starved and weary of frontier life. Teague was one of two Masons who bid to design the temple. He won, took over from his rival as grand super-intendent of works, then became grand master of Victoria's Masonic lodge, and eventually mayor of Victoria. He also designed City Hall. The Masons are still active in Victoria, their latest major project the housing that adjoins the temple on Fisgard Street.

Turn left (west) on Fisgard. Halfway down the block on the north side of the street is the Chinese School **(22)**, a direct result of anti-Oriental prejudice that decreed in 1907 that only Canadian-born Chinese children could at-tend public schools in the city. The Chinese Consolidated Benevolent Association had already lost a court suit chal-lenging a previous exclusionary ruling; now, they deter-mined to build their own school. The Zhonghua Xuetang (Chinese Imperial School) opened in 1909, with classes in English and Chinese. Now that Chinese Canadians are thoroughly integrated into the city's schools, the Chinese School offers after-school classes—to anyone, of any age or ethnic origin—in Chinese language and arts. The building itself is an interesting combination of western and oriental architectural forms.

Today's Chinatown begins here and stretches to Store Street on Fisgard, and for a block north and south. Historically, this was the heart of the Forbidden City, the

The Gee Tuck Tong Building in the 600-block Fisgard.

one part of Victoria where Chinese felt completely at home and whites rarely ventured. There are two sides to Chinatown today: the historic side, represented in the architecture and maze of courtyards and alleyways, and the modern side, seen in the restaurants, groceries, souvenir stores—and the artists' studios that now exist in the old tenement rooms above Fisgard Street.

Many Chinatown buildings were erected by tongs, groups of people with the same last name, or from the same geographic area of China, or speaking the same dialect, who came together for mutual benefit and protection in their new country. The beautifully restored building at 622–626 Fisgard was built by the Gee Tuck Tong in 1903. Next door, at 614 Fisgard, is the Lee Ben Association Building, from 1911.

Look at these buildings and others nearby for some of the characteristic architecture that joins Chinese tradition to western realities. Cheater storeys are mezzanines installed between first and second floors, a way around the tax collector who based assessments on floor space. Recessed balconies are common in southern China; warm in winter, cool in summer, they offer a vantage point to watch street activity. Traditional colours are everywhere: red symbolizes happiness; gold, wealth; yellow, the imperial power of China; green, peace, growth, harmony, or nature's bounty.

Continue west on Fisgard, across Government Street. Here, at the entrance to the busiest block of modern Chinatown, is *Tong Ji Men*, the Gate of Harmonious Interest **(23)**. It was erected in 1981 to symbolize the co-operation between Chinese Canadians and the rest of the community, and Chinese participation in the community. Look for the supernatural creatures who symbolize the quadrants of the heavenly vault in Chinese mythology: the azure dragon, the representative of the great celestial power and of the yang, or male, element of the universe; the vermilion phoenix, representing the ying, or female element; the white tiger; and the black tortoise.

Fan Tan Alley, in Chinatown.

The stone lions at the base of the gate were donated by Suzhou, Victoria's sister city in Jiangsu Province, China.

On either side of Fisgard **(24)**, between and behind buildings, are passages and courtyards that honeycomb these blocks. Wander into Fan Tan Alley (halfway down the block, on the south side). Fan Tan was once home to fan-tan gambling clubs, one of fourteen Victoria opium factories, and cafés and restaurants. Signs in Chinese characters mark the former sites of the fan-tan clubs. The alley was once closed off at both ends by a series of doors with peepholes that permitted Chinese to keep interlopers out. The upper storeys of these buildings were divided into tiny rooms, occupied mostly by elderly Chinese who came here from 1860 to 1914 to make money to send home to their families. Few could ever afford to return to China; few were allowed to bring their families to join them.

Chinatown today is a good place for a snack, breakfast, lunch, or dinner—or for souvenir or Oriental-food shopping. Try dim sum, a traditional lunch where servers wheel a multitude of dishes past your table and you point out what you want; noodle shops, with barbecued meats and steaming noodles; restaurants that serve Cantonese or spicier Szechuan food; barbecue shops that parcel out spicy duck or pork. Chinatown is not all about the Orient: a corner café serves cappuccino and latte.

Continue west on Fisgard, then turn left on Store Street. On your right is the old brick Janion Hotel, almost derelict now, built in 1891. On your left is the Lim Dat building (1898), and what was once a feed warehouse, now restored as a hotel, restaurant, and brewery.

The Harbourfront

Cross Pandora and continue to Wharf Street. Cross Johnson Street, then cross Wharf Street to the west (water) side. Turn left, to walk along the path beside Wharf Street (25). The two small buildings on your right, now

Would-be prospectors line up at the 1874 Dominion Customs Building on Wharf Street before they leave for the Klondike in about 1898. (BCARS 11581)

disused, were built as warehouses around 1865–70. **Just beyond these buildings, you'll see a tourism information sign on your left, a low wall on your right. Turn right to follow a pathway to water level. Turn left and follow the waterfront walkway (26) south, behind a modern multistorey hotel.**

Past the hotel on your left is the lower level of Hartwig Court, former warehouses whose random-rubble lower storeys fronted on the harbour to receive goods arriving by ship. Across a parking lot are bricked-up arches in a stone wall that rises to Wharf Street: this is the former site of the Hudson's Bay Company ware-house. The arches allowed entry to below-street storage.

Continue along the waterfront walkway (26). On your left, on the rocks past the parking lot, are the only remains of Fort Victoria: parts of mooring rings that were anchored in the rock. On your right all along here are docks where pleasure and fishing boats moor. The bright pink building with the mansard roof high on your left is the 1874 Dominion Customs Building.

Continue across the next parking lot to the left of the terminals for floatplanes to Vancouver and upcoast, and rejoin the waterfront walkway, keeping close to the docks. For a reminder of how things used to be, look for the *Robertson II* and the *Pacific Swift,* sloops owned by the Sail and Life Training Society, docked, if they are in port, at the south end of a water-level parking lot. You may also see, at appropriate times of the year, the huge seiners that fish for herring during the brief open-ings for that fishery, other fishboats, and large sailboats.

Keeping close to the water, follow the walkway to the eastern end of the Inner Harbour, then continue right (south) along the water (27). This section of the seawalk attracts buskers, civil servants on their lunch breaks, tourists enjoying the sunshine and the forest of masts in the Inner Harbour. **Climb the stairs at the south end of the harbour, to return to the walking tour start-ing point at Government and Belleville. (Wheelchair route: continue around the harbour, and follow the walkway to street level.)**

THE WESTSONG/
WEST BAY WALKWAY

THIS WALK BEGINS at the corner of Johnson and Wharf streets, at the east end of the Johnson Street Bridge (#25 on the map facing page 1). If you prefer to park beside the walkway, cross the Johnson Street Bridge heading away from downtown, then turn left at the first traffic lights, on Tyee Road. Follow Tyee around to a small parking area. To follow the tour in reverse, begin at the West Bay Marina, on Head Street in Esquimalt. You can drive to the marina, or take bus #25-Munro. Walkers find the Songhees end of the walkway particularly pleasant at dusk, when the lights of the buildings around the harbour come on, and the sunset is reflected in the water. It's probably not a good idea, though, to continue along the lonelier part of the walkway after dark.

From Johnson and Wharf streets, walk across the Johnson Street Bridge, double road and rail spans where the lifting span is counterbalanced by a weight at the other end of the bridge. While the road bridge was being built in 1922, one of the wooden caissons used in construction of the piers keeled over. But the engineer wasn't worried: the caisson was easily righted, "much to the evident chagrin of a large number of gentlemen of leisure who apparently spent their days wishing for bad luck to the rest of mankind." Sidewalk superintendents are ever with us.

A bleating horn signals to pedestrians and motorists that the span is about to lift to allow a boat to pass underneath; if you hear it as you are about to cross the bridge, prepare for a five-minute wait to permit a boat or ship to pass. A bridge operator keeps radio watch for approaching vessels.

Just past the end of the blue railing, bear left onto a walkway that skirts the water. When the Hudson's Bay Company built Fort Victoria in 1843, the Songhees band of Coast Salish Indians moved here from Cadboro Bay. The land was later designated as the Songhees Reserve. From 1859, city officials wanted the Songhees to move, so the city could use the land for industry, but the Songhees were securely in possession. In 1911, the Songhees agreed with federal and provincial governments that they would move to a new reserve, in Esquimalt, in return for the new land, cash, and a development fund. The deal later became a scandal, when it was discovered that people involved had billed the governments for almost as much as the Songhees got, and dark allegations of bribery emerged.

A walker on the Songhees pathways, with the M.V. Coho *leaving the harbour.*

For decades, oil-tank farms and various industries occupied Songhees. In the 1980s, the city sold much of the waterfront land for residential and hotel development.

It is 2.7 kilometres (about a mile and a half) along the water from the Johnson Street Bridge to the West Bay Marina. This section, skirting the Songhees development, was opened in 1990. A sign at the beginning of the walkway shows the route. On the low, rocky rise to your left as you follow the walkway are four concrete forms, once the foundations for a water tower that served Songhees industries.

The rocks provide a good viewpoint to watch harbour traffic. Seaplanes, scheduled, charter, and private, land at the entrance to the harbour, then taxi to docks at its head. The M.V. *Coho,* a grey-and-red American ferry, plies between Port Angeles, on the Olympic Peninsula across the Strait of Juan de Fuca, and downtown Victoria.

From various vantage points along the walkway, you can see Old Town as earlier travellers saw it, from the water side, and the Inner Harbour backed by the Empress Hotel and Parliament Buildings. To the right of the *Coho* dock is Laurel Point, once heavily industrial, now built up with condominiums and hotels. Fishboats tie up at Fishermen's Wharf, beyond Laurel Point. Still farther out is the Canadian coast guard station, with its red-and-white boats; the Ogden Point docks, with cruise liners or the occasional freighter tied up; and the breakwater that marks the end of the docks.

On this side of the harbour, you can see to the west the last remaining oil-tank farm at McLoughlin Point (wrongly spelled MacLaughlin on most maps) and the Work Point barracks and other military buildings. The military presence keeps alive the tradition established when the British navy made Esquimalt Harbour their headquarters on the Pacific coast in 1862. Dr. John McLoughlin and John Work were both esteemed employees of the Hudson's Bay Company.

As you follow the walkway, keep an eye out for a number of natural features. A variety of seabirds winter in these waters, among them herons, gulls, and kingfishers. Green-headed mallards and white-crowned wigeons paddle and dive, while cormorants, ungainly black birds with long bodies, large bills, and necks that curve in an S-shape, perch offshore on rocks and driftwood.

Offshore in a small cove along the walkway is a pole with nesting boxes attached. From April to August, look here for purple martins; the male of these big swallows is a bluish-purple. The Victoria Natural History Society has placed the boxes here to try to encourage the martins, which have traditionally nested in old pilings and which are increasingly rare in this area, to re-establish themselves.

At intervals, arbutus trees curve their smooth red trunks above the path. The only broad-leafed evergreen in British Columbia, the arbutus (known in the United

Arbutus trees and walkers on the Westsong walkway.

The Jacobson house, on Head Street near the West Bay Marina.

States as the madrona) sheds its papery bark, so tree trunks are often mottled green, red, orange, and brown.

A plaque about 1.5 kilometres along the walkway points out grooves in the rocks carved by an ice sheet that moved across the area fifteen thousand years ago.

The walkway ends at West Bay Marina, where pleasure boats and some liveaboards and houseboats are moored. As you look over the marina, you'll see a blue-and-white house crowned with a turret. Finnish sailor Victor Jacobson arrived dramatically at Victoria: he jumped ship—literally—and swam to shore, where he hid out until his ship left. He did well from his first few years in Victoria, and by the late 1880s owned a number of sealing and trading ships. He built the house at 507 Head

Street, overlooking West Bay Marina, in 1893, with the tower so positioned that he could watch for his sealers coming into harbour. Its shingles represent fish scales; the decorative trim is in the shape of hearts, flowers, butterflies, birds, stars, anchors, and ropes.

You can return along the walkway, or take public transit back to downtown. Bus #25-Munro stops just to the left of the walkway end, on Head Street, or you can walk three blocks to your right for more frequent bus service east along Esquimalt Road to downtown. In summer, a small ferry taxis people around the harbour, with stops at the marina, Songhees, downtown, and Laurel Point.

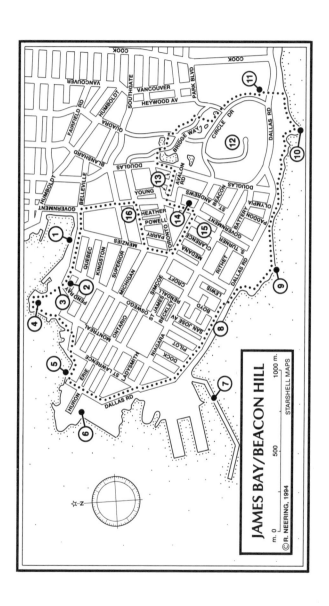

JAMES BAY/BEACON HILL

m. 0   500   1000 m.

© R. NEERING, 1994   STARSHELL MAPS

THE JAMES BAY/
BEACON HILL TOUR

THIS WALKING TOUR starts beside the Inner Harbour, then follows the waterfront around the Outer Harbour to the Dallas Road cliffs. It leads through Beacon Hill Park, then along residential James Bay streets back to the Legislative Precinct and the Inner Harbour. A circle, it is seven to eight kilometres long and relatively flat. The #5-Beacon Hill bus that leaves from and returns to downtown touches a number of points along the tour. Free parking is available along the waterfront and in Beacon Hill Park. Numbers in parentheses refer to the map on page 44.

The Harbourfront to Fishermen's Wharf

Begin at the northwest corner of Government and Belleville streets, beside the harbour, across from the Parliament Buildings. **Walk west—away from the Empress Hotel—along Belleville.** On your right, just before the Undersea Gardens and Wax Museum, is a plaque commemorating the 1825 treaty between Russia and Great Britain that fixed Canada's future boundaries, and noting the sea otter trade. The imposing and classical-looking building on your right **(1)** dates from the time when steamships crowded the harbour, carrying passengers to and from Vancouver, Vancouver Island points, and Seattle. The Canadian Pacific Navigation Company dominated the south side of the harbour from 1901 on, and built this steamship terminal in 1924. Look for heads of Poseidon, the Greek god of the sea, flanking the entrance of the building, now home to a wax museum. Just beyond the building, the American ferry M.V. *Coho,* plying between Victoria and Washington State, docks.

Continue west along Belleville Street. From the 1860s to the 1890s, James Bay was the most fashionable residential district in the city; some of the magnificent old houses still stand beside its streets. Two such are visible across Belleville Street, between Oswego and Pendray streets. Pleasantly austere, 327 Belleville (ca. 1877) was built for drygoods, tobacco, and liquor merchant A.B. Gray. William J. and Amelia Pendray's Loretto Hall at 309 Belleville **(2)** is certainly not austere; built in 1895, in a San Francisco style the couple had admired on their honeymoon, the house still dominates its surroundings, and the garden still reflects W.J.'s love of topiary.

Pendray noted when he arrived in Victoria in 1875

that Victorians paid top price for imported soaps while they threw out kitchen fat and tallow every day. From that realization came The British Columbia Soap Works, for "If people are ever to become contented, happy and prosperous, they first must be made clean." His soap factory and British American Paint Works dominated the Laurel Point shoreline for many years. But his success in business brought him little luck in his personal life. One of the Pendrays' four sons was killed almost outside their front door when a horse bolted; in 1913, part of a new fire-sprinkling system Pendray was inspecting in his factory broke, fell twelve metres, and killed him. Amelia lived on to 1937. The house was preserved because it was occupied by the Missionary Sisters of Notre Dame des Anges until the 1970s, when it became an inn.

Where Belleville Street curves left into Pendray Street, bear right onto a pathway (3) that leads toward the water. Continue on this pathway along the waterfront, keeping right wherever the path forks. Laurel Point **(4)** was industrial land for decades, with Pendray's two factories and others, wharves, and tank farms between here and Shoal Point. Laurel Point was redeveloped in the late 1970s, when condominium towers and a hotel were built. On your left beyond the hotel is a pavilion that commemorates Victoria's relationship with Morioka, its sister city in Japan.

Continue along the walkway, then turn left and climb the steps to Kingston Street just before the Coast Harbourside Hotel, as the waterfront pathway bears to

An early-morning fisherman checks out the menu at the Fishermen's Wharf café.

the right. Turn right on Kingston Street. Keep right as the street becomes St. Lawrence, then make an immediate right into Fishermen's Wharf (5).

The wharf leads an uncertain existence: since the 1960s, politicians have been promising changes and improvements at the wharf, now occupied by commercial fishing boats and a row of liveaboards and houseboats. Many Victorians want to see the wharves stay the way they are: the colourful boats and just as colourful residents, the chance to eat fish and chips to the rhythm of waves and boat wash, and the opportunity to buy fish and crabs right off the boat, all within sight of downtown, are worth a great deal.

Return to the street by turning left opposite the wharf office and walking out the wharf entrance onto Dallas Road. Follow Dallas Road along the waterfront.

Dallas Road

A Canadian coast guard station **(6)** occupies the land to the right, once the site of Victoria's first deep-sea wharves. When the fleet and opulent *Empress of India* arrived in Victoria in 1891, it was forced to anchor offshore, since it could not manoeuvre in the Inner Harbour. Merchant and former mayor Robert Rithet was aggrieved by this; he was also convinced that Victoria must have wharves that would accommodate the large new ocean-going ships if it were to compete with brash young Vancouver. He had Rithet's Wharves constructed; they were replaced by the Ogden Point Docks in 1914.

You'll often see at the coast guard station the conical red and green buoys used to mark channels in B.C. rivers and along the province's coasts. Two retired buoys are displayed outside the station. The five-foot conical red buoy anchored to a stone setting by a chain dates to 1896. The nine-and-a-half-foot green electrical buoy (note the light on top) is also of an outmoded type.

Farther along between road and water are a helijet pad (service to Vancouver) and the Ogden Point Docks, once home to a cold-storage fish plant and a grain elevator. Victoria's only deep-sea wharves, they now serve

Pathways on the cliffs beside Dallas Road.

cruise ships, occasional freighters, and the *Royal Victorian,* a ferry that sails the Victoria-Seattle route.

Two houses on the other side of Dallas Road rate a glance. The middle-class house at 90–92 Dallas was built in 1906–7. The ca. 1894 brick house at 138 Dallas was built for Charles Newcombe, a doctor by profession, who travelled the coast studying geology and botany, and who worked with and studied the native peoples. For better or worse, he shipped much native art to the museums of the world. When his son died in 1960, the provincial museum bought the magnificent Newcombe collection.

The breakwater **(7)** marks the end of Victoria's harbour. This eight-hundred-metre-long pier breaks the force of the strong southeasterlies that batter the cliffs. It was built in 1919 of concrete and great slabs of granite. Although it still protects the harbour, Victorians are more likely to think of the breakwater as a place to walk, run, or fish.

Continue along Dallas Road (8). You may well see divers edging into the water here: this area is rich in undersea life and has been declared a federal submarine reserve, off-limits to underwater fishers or hunters.

Bear right onto the path that follows the cliffs around Holland Point (9). Where the path veers away from the road, a cairn recalls the shipwreck of the steam collier S.S. *San Pedro,* on Brotchie Ledge, a major hazard for ships entering Victoria's harbour. Ironically, the *San Pedro* was wrecked in clear calm weather while dropping off its pilot. The flashing light atop a white pillar just offshore marks the ledge.

Habitation atop these cliffs long predates Fort Victoria. Watchers in a strategically placed, fortified Coast Salish village could alert the village to interlopers coming across the Strait of Juan de Fuca. Native burial grounds were also located along the cliff tops.

As the path returns toward Dallas Road, a sign points to Fonyo Beach, at the foot of Paddon Avenue. In May of 1985, six thousand Victorians crowded along the waterfront to welcome Steve Fonyo, a one-legged nineteen-year-old who ran and walked 7924 kilometres across Canada to raise $9 million for cancer research. Fonyo emptied a jar of Atlantic Ocean water into the Pacific to conclude his run.

At the foot of Olympia Avenue, a cairn marks the former location of the Victoria Point Battery, two 64-pounder guns placed in 1878 to guard against an expected Russian invasion. As the Victoria *Colonist* reported after war broke out between Russia and Turkey, "much anxiety continues to be felt here regarding the defenceless nature of our coast," a fear apparently stemming from the Crimean War, twenty-five years earlier, that pitted Russia against Britain. A few years later, the fears were re-awoken when a well-dressed Russian was reported to be checking on Victoria's defences. But the journey across the Pacific must have had scant appeal, for the Russians never showed up.

The pathway curves back toward Dallas Road, at the foot of Douglas Street. Across Dallas Road are two commemorative plaques, one marking Steve Fonyo's marathon, the second Victoria long-distance runner Al Howie's 1991 seventy-three-day cross-Canada trek to raise money for special-needs children. Mile 0—never converted to Kilometre 0—of the 7821-kilometre Trans-Canada Highway, formally opened in 1962, is also located here.

Follow the pathway away from the road toward Finlayson Point (10). A sign here, evidence of a continuing battle fought in the letters-to-the-editor column of the Victoria newspaper, outlines rules governing dogs and their walkers. The battle is between those who love to see dogs run free and those who are annoyed when said unleashed dogs nip at their heels, cannon into children, fight with other dogs, or leave odorous evidence of their presence.

The Salish called this area the Bay of Falling Cliffs; a glance across the cove will show you why. Left to itself, the cliff edge would gradually erode, pushing the shoreline back toward the city. City workers are trying to halt this process as unobtrusively and naturally as possible. An artificial reef is being built offshore; workers are spiking vegetation like that already found on the more stable cliffs into the less stable ones, hoping the network of roots will hold the soil together. The effects of the weather are visible also in the wind-sculpted brush along the cliffs and the stunted trees.

Near the "1-km" sign, the path emerges into a meadow with Beacon Hill visible to your left. The hill is named for the twin beacons that flashed from the hilltops, navigational aids to mariners seeking entrance to the harbour around the dangers of Brotchie Ledge. On the right is a stone plinth to the twinning of Victoria and Morioka, Japan, and to the memory of Dr. Inazo Nitobe, a native of Morioka, dedicated to the cause of peace, who died in Victoria in 1933. Inscribed on the monument are Nitobe's words, "It is my wish to serve as a bridge over the Pacific Ocean."

Look down from the cliffs at Horseshoe Bay, marked by a sign, to see evidence of glaciation thousands of years ago. Near Finlayson Point is a plaque commemorating Roderick Finlayson, chief factor at Fort Victoria from its founding to 1872. Also at Finlayson Point, a Salish village once stood. A second gun installation was meant to deter (obviously successfully, since they never attacked) Russian invaders.

The early 1950s were the era of the marathon swimmers, challenging Lake Ontario, the English Channel— and the Strait of Juan de Fuca. Although an American was the first to swim the strait, Marilyn Bell, who hit the headlines when she made the first crossing of Lake Ontario in 1954, was the first woman, the first Canadian, and the youngest person to swim the Strait of Juan de Fuca. She did so in 1956, at the age of seventeen. A cairn points out her landing place.

Beacon Hill Park

Just past the fifteen-hundred-metre post, at the end of a wooded area, turn left on a pathway that leads to a crosswalk across Dallas Road. Cross Dallas, and walk to the totem pole (11) in front of you. This Kwakwaka'wakw pole, carved by artists from Fort Rupert on the northern tip of Vancouver Island, was known as the tallest in the world, but that honour now belongs to a pole in Kwakwaka'wakw territory.

You are in Beacon Hill Park **(12)**, named for the hill to your left. Much of the seventy-four-hectare green space was reserved as park land by James Douglas in the 1850s. Long home to sports such as cricket, horse racing, and field lacrosse, the park now has cricket and other sports fields, tennis courts, a lawn-bowling green, and a pitch-and-putt golf course. It's a favourite with families who feed the ducks, visit the children's farm,

Pre-1900 gardeners set to work at Beacon Hill Park. (BCARS 12000)

and picnic in the park. Much of the park is left in a semi-wild state, with Douglas fir, ferns, and Garry oaks prominent among the rocks and meadows.

Turn right at the park road, and walk along its edge, across the next two roads. On your right, somewhat hidden in the shrubbery, are a plaque and bust of Queen

Elizabeth II, who visited Victoria in 1959. Beyond are the park's rose gardens. **Continue past Queen's Lake.** On your left is the children's farm, complete with peacocks, farm animals, and a commemoration of Queenie, the Clydesdale horse that entertained children from 1950 to 1970. A series of boards beside the farm displays park maps and pictures of birds you may encounter in the park.

Turn right across a humpbacked bridge that crosses Deer Lake. Look to the left to see the floral wagonwheel. **Continue along the path to the road, cross the road toward the park service building and public washrooms, and turn left. Follow the edge of the road, past the children's playground.**

Here and elsewhere in the park you will see Garry oaks, the characteristically twisted and craggy trees that grow in rocky meadows, now threatened by disease and development, but bolstered by a city-wide preservation and planting effort. If parks staff have their way, you will see more Garry oaks and less broom, the yellow-flowered invader that spread from a few seeds brought to Victoria by a Scottish settler to a dominant species in the open spaces of the southern island. Gardeners are ripping out the broom, hoping to encourage native species to re-establish.

Continue along the road, bearing right where it forks at Bridge Way, then cross the road and follow the pathway to the left, along the south shore of Goodacre Lake, an artificial pond created in 1889–90 and later named for the city councillor and butcher who donated much of the meat for zoo animals. **Go up the steps (wheelchairs, keep left, then right) and turn right at the next road, to cross a stone bridge** built in 1889 to resemble a rustic medieval bridge. **Turn left at the end of the bridge. Follow the path along the lake, then cross the grass to your right and turn left on Douglas Street. Cross Douglas Street at the crosswalk that leads to Avalon Road and walk down Avalon.**

Residential James Bay

These two blocks of Avalon Road **(13)** and the intersecting block of Huntington Place contain a half-dozen heritage houses built between 1890 and 1907 for middle-class businessmen: a contractor, a printer, a druggist, several artisans, a merchant, a dentist. Look for the widow's walk atop 613 Avalon, gingerbread detailing, and bow windows. Several of the houses have been recently restored.

Cross on the pedestrian pathway at the end of Avalon to Government Street, and turn left. Across the street is the James Bay Inn, built in 1911 as a quiet retreat for the weary traveller, with "ample space between it and the surrounding property to secure light and fresh air in unlimited quantity." Artist and writer Emily Carr, an unparalleled painter of the totems and wilderness of the west coast, spent her last years here, in a back room just a block from where she was born. That house, down the

The Carr House in the 200-block Government Street.

block at 207 Government **(14)**, was built for Emily's father Richard and mother Emily after they arrived in Victoria in 1862 with their two daughters. Known now as the Emily Carr House, the building has been restored and is open to the public, as a Victorian period piece.

Two routes are possible here. To see a cluster **(15)** of restored and unrestored residences from the turn of the century, **continue south on Government, turn right on Niagara, right on South Turner, then left on Simcoe**. For a shorter route from the Carr house, **turn right on Simcoe from Government Street and walk west.**

The house one down from the southwest corner of Simcoe and Clarence streets was built in about 1885. Some years later, William Wallace Gibson moved in, and began fooling around in the back yard. Gibson had been fascinated by flight since he had flown a kite during his Saskatchewan boyhood. He made money on a gold claim, and decided to try his hand at aviation. In his back yard and shed, Gibson put together the first all-Canadian airplane, which he later said "jumped around like a chicken with its head cut off." The Gibson Twin Plane, powered by a four-cylinder, two-cycle, fifty-horsepower engine, flew sixty-one metres before Gibson grounded it because he didn't want to crash into some nearby trees. Gibson later gave up his flying experiments, and moved to the United States, where he did well designing mining machinery.

Continue west along Simcoe Street. The sign for the Beckley Farm Lodge, an extended-care home, is the last reminder of a time when much of James Bay was the Beckley Farm, run by the Hudson's Bay Company.

Turn right on Menzies Street. Near the corner formed by Menzies, Simcoe, and Toronto streets are several turn-of-the-century buildings, including 512 Simcoe, built by Hudson's Bay Company factor John Chandler in 1884. This area, with its shops and services, is the centre of present-day James Bay, with its population of single people, retired apartment dwellers, civil servants, and professionals who have restored the old cottages and mansions.

Continue north on Menzies to Michigan Street and turn right, past the James Bay United Church, dedicated in 1892. The blocks to the north and east are part of the Legislative Precinct, which contains a mixture of heritage houses, office blocks, and government buildings intended

Details of the Robson house at Michigan and Government streets.

as temporary when they were built. If the provisions of the Victoria Accord, between the provincial and city governments, go through, it will face radical change. Temporary office buildings will be torn down, heritage buildings moved, and some two hundred residences, fifty thousand square metres of office space, retail space, parking, and various services will be built.

The plans concern many James Bay residents, who worry about increased density, traffic, and noise, and some in private enterprise, who want government to stay out of the building business.

Until the changes occur, the heritage buildings remain. Take a look at the ones on the north side of Michigan Street, now housing various government departments. **Turn left on Government Street.** The house on the corner, at 506 Government **(16)**, was built in 1885 for John Robson, pioneer New Westminster newspaperman, fervent supporter of the Canadian cause, and premier of British Columbia from 1889 to 1892. He died in office, of blood poisoning, after he caught his finger in the door of a hansom cab in England. Next door, at 514 Government, lived Robson's daughter and son-in-law, Joseph Hunter. This mirror image of the Robson house was built so that mother and daughter could enjoy daily visits.

Continue north on Government Street, to return to the starting point of this walking tour at Government and Belleville streets.

FURTHER READING

Castle, Geoffrey, and Barry F. King. *Victoria Landmarks*. Victoria: self-published, 1985.

————. *More Victoria Landmarks*. Victoria: Sono Nis Press, 1988. Details and anecdotes on heritage and historic sites.

Kluckner, Michael. *Victoria The Way It Was*. Vancouver: Whitecap Books, 1986. Loving detail on old Victoria.

Lai, David Chuenyan. *The Forbidden City within Victoria*. Victoria: Orca Books, 1991. Fascinating information on Chinatown, then and now.

Segger, Martin, and Douglas Franklin. *Victoria: A History in Architecture*. Victoria: Heritage Architectural Guides, 1979. Background on Victoria's heritage buildings.

This Old House. Victoria: City of Victoria, 1979. A heritage report on residential Victoria.

This Old Town. Victoria: City of Victoria, 1983. Heritage in Old Town.